LOOKING AT THE NIGHT SKY

Written by
Clare Oliver and Adam Hibbert
Illustrated by
Mike Lacey, Terry Riley and Stephen Sweet

p

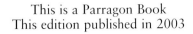

This is a Parragon Book
This edition published in 2003

Parragon
Queen Street House
4 Queen Street
Bath BA1 1HE, UK

Copyright © Parragon 2001

Original book created by

David West 👫 Children's Books

British Library Cataloguing-in-Publication Data

A catalogue record for this book is available from the British Library.

ISBN 1-40540-276-8

Printed in Dubai, U.A.E

Designers
Aarti Parmar
Rob Shone
Fiona Thorne
Illustrators
John Butler
Jim Eldridge
James Field
Andrew & Angela Harland
Colin Howard
Rob Jakeway
Mike Lacey
Sarah Lees
Gilly Marklew
Dud Moseley
Terry Riley
Sarah Smith
Stephen Sweet
Mike Taylor
Ross Watton
(SGA)
Ian Thompson
Cartoonist
Peter Wilks
(SGA)
Editor
James Pickering
Consultant
Steve Parker

CONTENTS

4 Who gazes at the stars?

5 Can anyone be an astronomer?

5 Can you only see the Moon and stars at night?

6 Who built a tomb for the Sun god?

6 Who built a stone circle for the Sun?

7 Who thought the sky was a goddess?

8 Who first wrote about the stars?

9 How do we know about the first astronomers?

9 What was a Babylonian year like?

10 Who thought the Sun was as wide as a ruler?

11 Who named groups of stars?

11 Who worked out the Earth is round?

12 Why do stars make patterns?

12 What is the zodiac?

13 Which stars make a hunter?

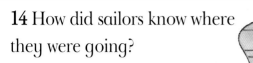

14 How did sailors know where they were going?

15 How did an astrolabe work?

15 What is the pole star?

16 Who made the first telescope?

17 How does a telescope work?

17 Who put mirrors in a telescope?

18 Who said that planets go round the Sun?

18 Who was put on trial for star-gazing?

19 Who first used a telescope for astronomy?

20 Where do astronomers put their telescopes?

20 Where's the best place to build an observatory?

21 How can a telescope see through the roof?

22 How deep is space?

22 Are there candles in space?

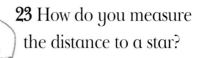

23 How do you measure the distance to a star?

24 Who made the first radio telescope?

24 Which are the most powerful radio telescopes?

25 Where is the biggest radio telescope?

26 What's a gravity telescope?

26 Can we see black holes?

27 What's the weirdest telescope?

28 Are there telescopes in space?

28 Are there observatories in space?

29 Which telescope is in orbit?

30 What's better than a powerful telescope?

31 Could we build Very Large Arrays in space?

31 Could we build an observatory on the Moon?

32 Glossary and Index

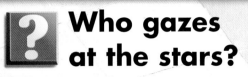

? Who gazes at the stars?

We all enjoy looking up at the starry night sky, especially on a clear moonless night, away from bright city lights. Some people even star-gaze as a job. They are scientists called astronomers. Astronomy is the science of studying space and all the objects in it.

4

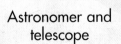
Astronomer and telescope

Amazing! You can see about 2,500 stars in the night sky! When the sky is clear, you can see that many different stars even without a telescope!

Can anyone be an astronomer?

Anyone can learn about stars as a hobby, but it takes years of study to do it as a job. You'll need books of star charts and maps, so you can recognise what you see. Binoculars or a telescope will let you see further.

Studying a star chart

Is it true?
You can see the Moon's craters through binoculars.

Yes. Binoculars allow you to see the Moon's surface so clearly that you can make out individual craters – from 400,000 km away!

Can you only see the Moon and stars at night?

The Moon and stars are easiest to spot, but even without a telescope you will see meteors (shooting stars) and the brighter planets, such as Venus, Jupiter or Mars. Venus shines white and is nicknamed the 'evening star'. Jupiter looks greeny-blue and Mars glows red.

Meteor shower

Who built a tomb for the Sun god?

The Ancient Egyptians thought their kings were the Sun god, Re, who had come down to Earth. They buried kings in huge tombs called pyramids, maybe because the pyramid shape pointed at the sky.

Pyramid

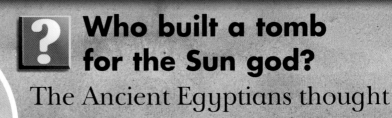

Who built a stone circle for the Sun?

No one knows exactly why Stonehenge, a huge stone circle in southwest England, was built by Druids over 4,000 years ago. Its doorway would have framed the sunrise on the longest day of each year.

Is it true?
Stonehenge was a primitive computer.

No. But in the 1960s an American scientist called Gerald Hawkins said it was. He thought Stonehenge was built to work out when eclipses would happen.

6

Ancient Druid ceremony at Stonehenge

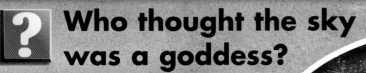

? Who thought the sky was a goddess?

The Egyptians thought the night sky was the arched body of a goddess, called Nut. Today we know Nut's body matches the view of the Milky Way from Ancient Egypt.

The Milky Way seen above the pyramids

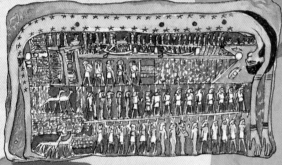

Ancient Egyptian wall painting showing the goddess Nut

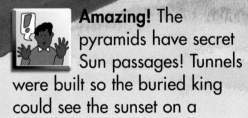

Amazing! The pyramids have secret Sun passages! Tunnels were built so the buried king could see the sunset on a particular day each spring.

7

Who first wrote about the stars?

The Babylonians were the first to write down their findings from studying the stars – around 5,000 years ago! They noticed that stars seem to form patterns, which we call constellations. The Babylonian empire was roughly where Iraq is today.

Babylonian astromomers

Is it true?
The Babylonians were maths wizards.

Yes. At first their findings about the night sky were based on looking and guessing. By around 500 BC, the Babylonians used sums to predict exactly when events such as eclipses would happen.

8

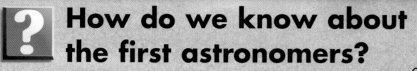

? How do we know about the first astronomers?

The Babylonians didn't write on paper like we do. They wrote on clay tablets, so fragments have survived. Scientists called archaeologists dig in the ground for clues about ancient peoples such as the Babylonians.

Babylonian writing on a clay tablet

Amazing! The Babylonians didn't see the same night sky as us. There were no twinkling satellites, and the stars were in different places because our Solar System has moved since then.

? What was a Babylonian year like?

The Babylonians worked out a 12-month year. Each month began with the first sight of the crescent Moon. The months were called Nisannu, Ayaru, Simanu, Du'uzu, Abu, Ululu, Tashritu, Arahsamnu, Kislimu, Tebetu, Shabatu and Addaru.

Clay tablet

9

10

Amazing! An eclipse changed the course of history. Soldiers from Athens in Ancient Greece lost a battle after being spooked by an eclipse of the Moon. Their rivals, the Spartans, were the winners.

? Who thought the Sun was as wide as a ruler?

The Greek thinker Heraclitus thought the Sun was just 30 cm across and that a new one was made each morning. So even though the Ancient Greeks were clever, they didn't get everything right!

Heraclitus

Who named groups of stars?

In AD 150, the Greek astronomer Ptolemy wrote a book about the stars, describing 48 different constellations (star groups). He named the groups after characters from Greek myths, such as Perseus, the hero who rescued the princess Andromeda. We still use Ptolemy's names today.

Perseus and Andromeda

Is it true?
People once thought the Earth was flat.

Yes. Even up to the 1500s most people believed this. They thought that if you sailed too far, you could fall off the edge!

Aristotle

Who worked out the Earth is round?

The Ancient Greek thinker Aristotle realised that the Earth must be round in the 330s BC. He worked this out when he was watching a lunar eclipse, because he saw that the Earth made a circular shadow on the surface of the Moon.

? Why do stars make patterns?

Constellations are the patterns that bright stars seem to make in the night sky, such as a cross, a letter 'W' or the shape of a person. The stars look close together – but that's just how we see them from Earth. Really they are scattered through space and nowhere near each other.

Amazing! The night sky is divided into 88 different star patterns. Nearly 50 were first described 2,000 years ago!

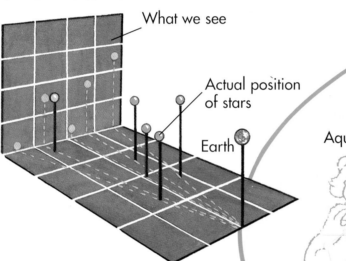

What we see

Actual position of stars

Earth

Aquarius

Sagittarius

Virgo

Libra

Capricornus

Scorpius

Zodiac constellations

? What is the zodiac?

For astronomers, the zodiac includes the 12 constellations that the Sun passes through during a year. We can't see the Sun doing this, though. The Sun's light is so bright that we cannot see the constellations during the day.

12

Which stars make a hunter?

Orion is a constellation named after the legendary Greek hunter. Lots of stars make up the shape. Rigel is the brightest and makes one of the hunter's legs. The next-brightest is Betelgeuse, which shines a reddish colour.

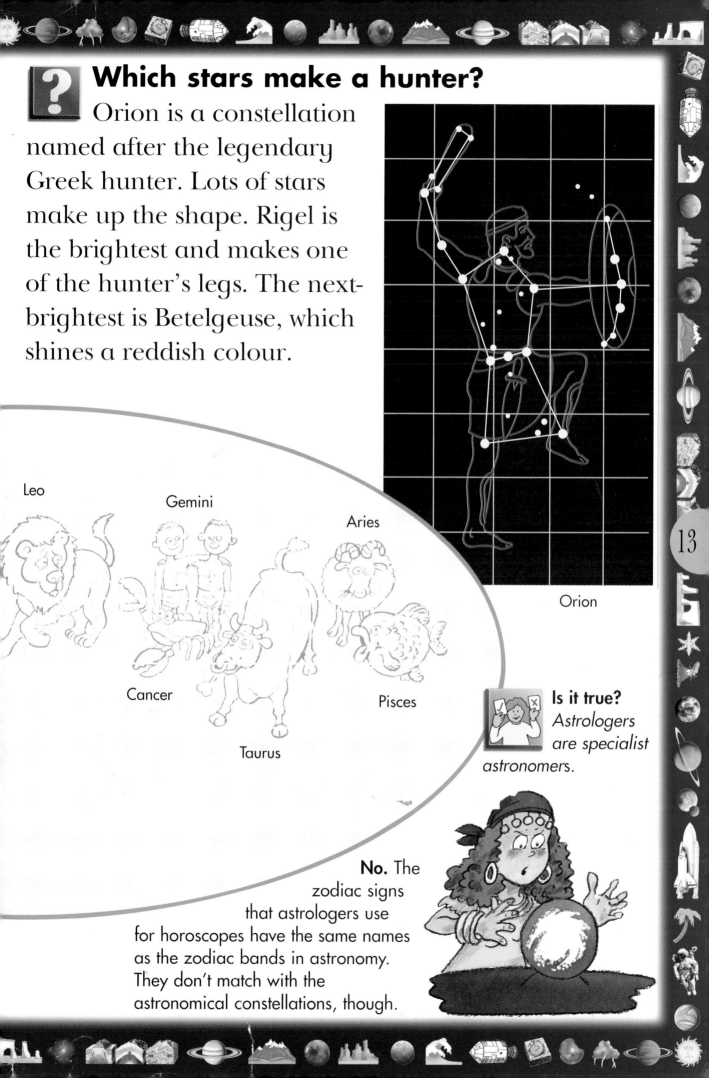

Orion

Leo

Gemini

Aries

Cancer

Pisces

Taurus

13

Is it true?
Astrologers are specialist astronomers.

No. The zodiac signs that astrologers use for horoscopes have the same names as the zodiac bands in astronomy. They don't match with the astronomical constellations, though.

? How did sailors know where they were going?

Out at sea, there are no landmarks. In the Middle Ages, sailors had special instruments that used the position of the Sun and stars to tell them where they were. These included compasses, astrolabes and cross-staffs.

Sailor and cross-staff

Amazing! The first astrolabes were made 1,500 years ago! Indian and Arab astronomers used pocket-sized instruments called astrolabes in the AD 500s.

Is it true?
Astrolabes only worked at night.

No. You could use the position of the Sun instead of the stars, when you were sailing during the day. You looked at its position compared to the horizon.

How did an astrolabe work?

An astrolabe had two discs, one with a star map, and the other with measuring lines and a pointer. You compared them with the Sun or a star and the horizon to work out your position.

Astrolabe

What is the pole star?

The only star which doesn't appear to move is above the North Pole. Sailors could tell where they were by looking at the pole star – it's lowest in the sky at the Equator.

Path of the stars with the pole star in the middle

15

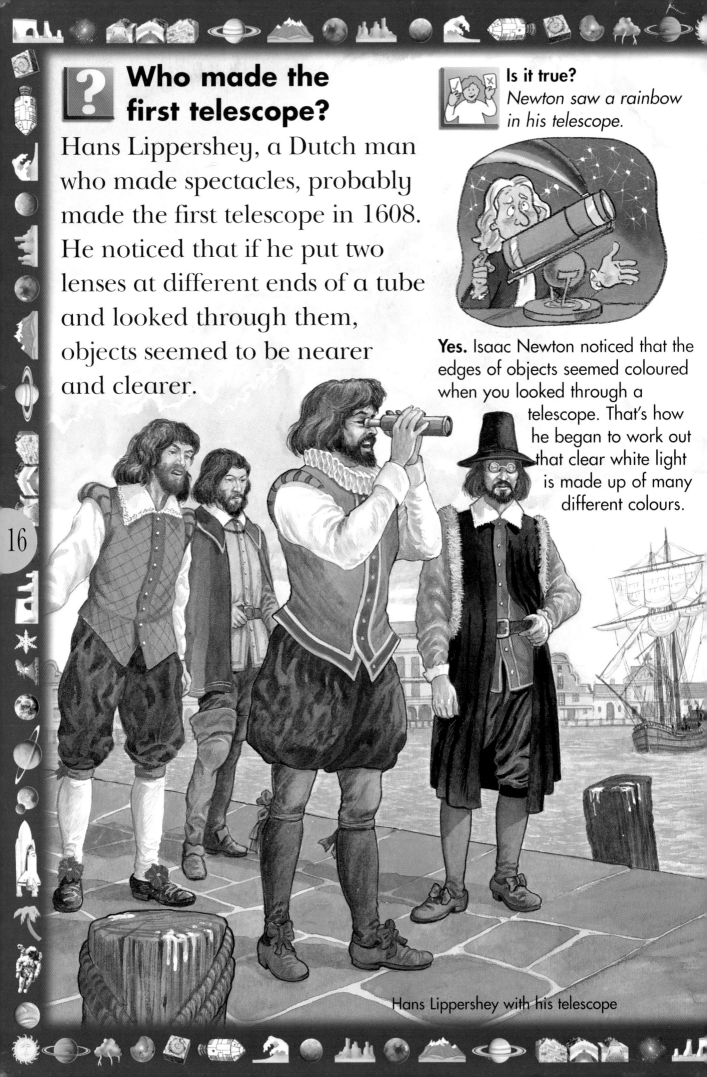

Who made the first telescope?

Hans Lippershey, a Dutch man who made spectacles, probably made the first telescope in 1608. He noticed that if he put two lenses at different ends of a tube and looked through them, objects seemed to be nearer and clearer.

Is it true?

Newton saw a rainbow in his telescope.

Yes. Isaac Newton noticed that the edges of objects seemed coloured when you looked through a telescope. That's how he began to work out that clear white light is made up of many different colours.

Hans Lippershey with his telescope

How does a telescope work?

The lens (curved piece of glass) at the front end of a telescope gathers light to make an image of an object that is far away. The lens at the back magnifies the image so it can be seen more clearly.

Simple cutaway of a telescope

Who put mirrors in a telescope?

Isaac Newton was the first person to make a mirror or reflecting telescope. He replaced the front lens with a dish-shaped mirror at the back. The mirror reflected the image on to a smaller mirror, and then into the eye.

Newton's reflecting telescope

Amazing! You can see Saturn's rings through a telescope. Telescopes magnify images (make them bigger) so much that you can even make out Saturn's faint rings – which are about 1.3 billion km away!

Who said that planets go round the Sun?

Nicolaus Copernicus explained this idea in a book in 1543. The problem was, the Church stated that God had put the Earth at the centre of the Universe. You could be put to death for saying that the Earth went round the Sun.

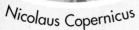

Nicolaus Copernicus

Who was put on trial for star-gazing?

Few scientists were brave enough to say that they agreed with Copernicus's findings that the Earth went round the Sun. The Italian astronomer Galileo was – and was put on trial for his ideas in 1634.

Is it true?
The Church accepted that Galileo was right in the end.

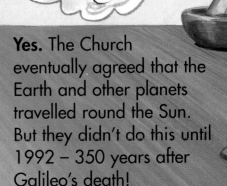

Yes. The Church eventually agreed that the Earth and other planets travelled round the Sun. But they didn't do this until 1992 – 350 years after Galileo's death!

Galileo on trial

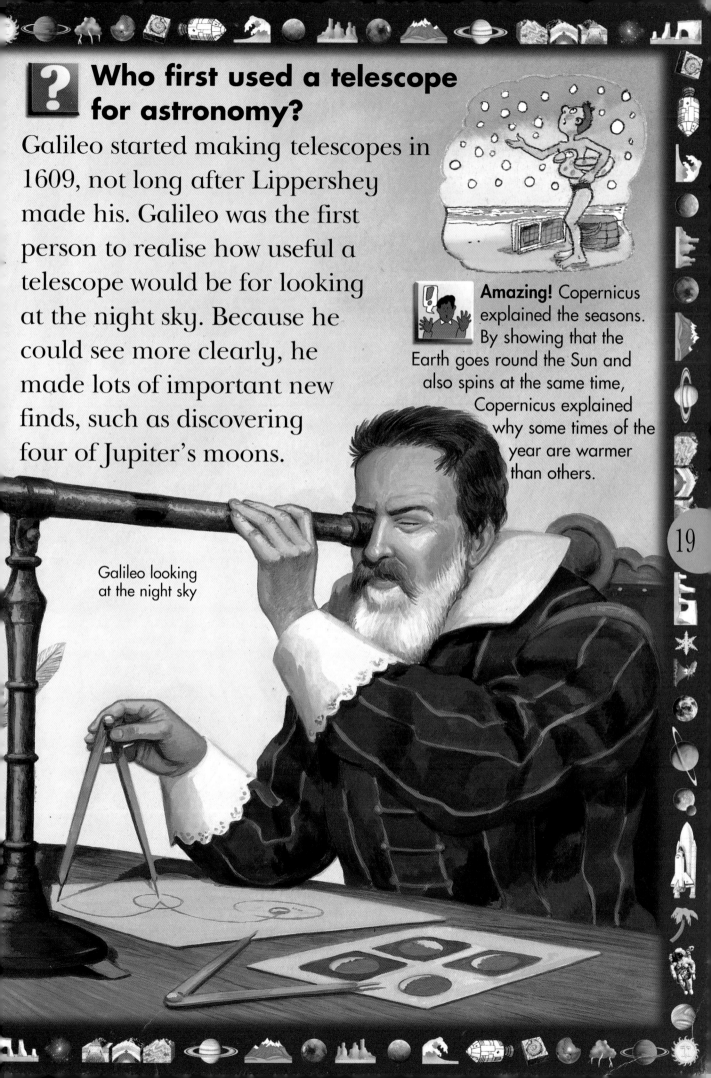

? Who first used a telescope for astronomy?

Galileo started making telescopes in 1609, not long after Lippershey made his. Galileo was the first person to realise how useful a telescope would be for looking at the night sky. Because he could see more clearly, he made lots of important new finds, such as discovering four of Jupiter's moons.

Amazing! Copernicus explained the seasons. By showing that the Earth goes round the Sun and also spins at the same time, Copernicus explained why some times of the year are warmer than others.

Galileo looking at the night sky

Where do astronomers put their telescopes?

Observatories are buildings where astronomers go to look at the sky. They house the most powerful telescopes on Earth. The telescopes are usually kept in a room with a dome-shaped roof. Observatories have other instruments too, such as very precise clocks, to help keep accurate time and records.

Pulkovo Observatory, Russia

Mount Cerro Observatory, Chile

Where's the best place to build an observatory?

Where you'll get the clearest view! Most are built away from city lights. Mountain-tops are best of all, because they poke above any clouds that might spoil the view.

Is it true?
The Greenwich Observatory houses the most telescopes.

No. The Kitt Peak National Observatory in Arizona, USA has the most optical telescopes. One of them, the Mayall Telescope, is 4 m across!

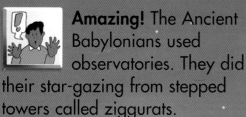
Amazing! The Ancient Babylonians used observatories. They did their star-gazing from stepped towers called ziggurats.

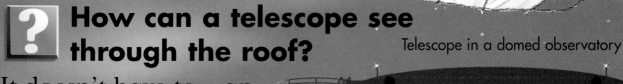

? How can a telescope see through the roof?

Telescope in a domed observatory

21

It doesn't have to – an observatory's domed roof is specially designed to slide open at night, so that the picture through the telescope isn't distorted (blurred) by looking through a window. The telescope can be pointed at any place in the sky.

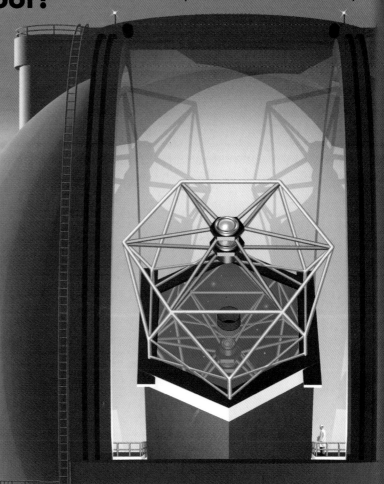

How deep is space?

Early astronomers thought that all the stars were the same distance from us, forming a simple shell around the Earth. Now we know that some stars are relatively close to us, and others are trillions of kilometres away.

Amazing! Galaxies move so quickly they are different colours. The light waves from them change, just as a fire engine's siren sounds lower after it zooms past. We use the colour to measure the galaxies' speed.

Gaseous clouds in deep space

Are there candles in space?

Not really. But we can see how far away a galaxy is by the brightness of a special type of star, called a 'standard candle'. The further away the galaxy, the dimmer the candle.

? How do you measure the distance to a star?

Watch the tip of your finger as you move it towards to your nose. The closer it gets, the more cross-eyed you become! Astronomers can tell the distance to a star by measuring how 'cross-eyed' a pair of telescopes has to be to see it.

Is it true?
We measure how far the stars are in kilometres.

NEAREST STAR
40 000 000 000 000 KM

No. They're so far away, that we use light years instead. A light year is how far light travels in one year – 9,461 billion km!

Who made the first radio telescope?

Radio telescopes are like giant satellite dishes that pick up invisible radio waves and similar waves, instead of light rays. Unlike light, radio waves can travel through cloud, so radio telescopes can be built just about anywhere! An American called Grote Reber made the first one in the 1930s.

Reber's radio telescope was a simple metal frame.

Amazing! A telescope can be 8,000 km long. The Very Long Baseline Array (VLBA) stretches across the USA. It has ten different dishes and produces the best-quality radio images of space from Earth yet!

Which are the most powerful radio telescopes?

The ones that are made up of several different radio dishes, such as the Very Large Array (VLA) in New Mexico, USA. The VLA has 27 dishes, each 25 metres across. Scientists compare the findings from all 27 dishes to get super-accurate results.

VLA, Socorro, New Mexico

Where is the biggest radio telescope?

The world's biggest single-dish radio telescope was built in Puerto Rico in the Caribbean about 40 years ago. It is 300 metres across – so it would take you more than ten minutes to walk around the edge of it.

Radio telescope, Puerto Rico

Is it true?
Only ten astronomers are allowed to use the VLA.

No. It is used by over 500 astronomers a year. Some study our near-neighbours in the Solar System, while others peer way beyond our galaxy to others in deepest space.

Gravity telescope

? What's a gravity telescope?

A gravity telescope uses laser beams to measure its own length. As a gravity wave passes through Earth from space, it stretches the telescope by less than the width of an atom! Four huge gravity telescopes were built at the end of the 1990s.

Amazing! The biggest gravity wave telescope is 4 km long! No one knows yet what new things gravity wave telescopes will help astronomers discover.

26

? Can we see black holes?

We can through a gravity telescope. Although light can't escape a black hole, gravity can. When a black hole swallows up a star, for example, there's a 'ripple' of gravity through space. Gravity wave telescopes spot the ripples.

Black hole

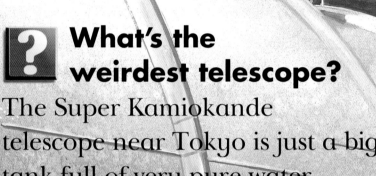

❓ What's the weirdest telescope?

The Super Kamiokande telescope near Tokyo is just a big tank full of very pure water, buried deep underground. Very sensitive cameras detect teeny-weeny particles called neutrinos zooming through the Earth, by recording microscopic flashes of light in the water.

Neutrino detector

Is it true?
Neutrinos have a dark secret.

Yes. Scientists think the Universe is full of something heavy, which they call dark matter. Neutrinos may be part of it!

Are there telescopes in space?

Yes – the first one went up in the 1960s. Space is a perfect place for looking at the stars. The sky is always dark and cloudless. Away from Earth's pollution and wobbly atmosphere, the stars shine steadily and brightly, instead of twinkling as they do to us on Earth.

28

X-ray multi-mirror telescope

Are there observatories in space?

Yes – some observatories use powerful gamma rays, which can penetrate all the gas and dust in the galaxy, to show us what is happening in its centre. The Compton gamma ray observatory was launched into space by the shuttle.

Gamma ray observatory

Which telescope is in orbit?

The most famous is the Hubble Space Telescope, which was carried into orbit on the space shuttle Discovery in 1990. It circles the Earth every 90 minutes, about 600 km above us. It beams radio signals of information to astronomers on Earth.

Hubble Space Telescope

Is it true?
Telescopes can look back in time.

Yes. Because of the time it takes X-rays to travel through space, Chandra can see quasars as they were ten billion years ago!

Amazing! Hubble runs on Sun-power. Hubble's two 'paddles' are solar panels. They gather energy from the Sun and change it into electrical energy. The energy is used to focus the telescope and beam data home.

❓ What's better than a powerful telescope?

Seeing for yourself in close-up – but it's too dangerous and expensive to send astronomers deep into space. That's why space probes are such important tools. Space probes are fitted with cameras. They beam back close-up photos of faraway planets and comets.

Cassini-Huygens
spacecraft

Amazing! Chandra is a billion times more powerful than the first X-ray telescope. If telescopes keep improving at this rate, we'll be able to see the farthest edges of the Universe in 30 years' time!

Is it true?
A probe found a watery world.

Yes. The Voyager 2 probe photographed what might be water on Jupiter's moon, Europa. If there is life out there, probes will probably find it first.

Could we build Very Large Arrays in space?

Scientists are already testing a cluster of satellites that fly in perfect formation, using laser beams. The same technology will be used to create a string of small satellite telescopes, making one huge 'eye' in space.

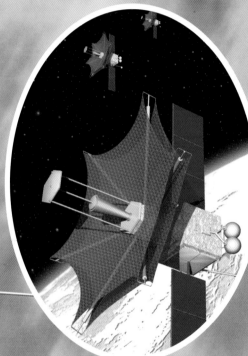

VLA in space

Could we build an observatory on the Moon?

The dark side of the Moon would be a perfect site. Always pointing away from the Earth, it is shielded from man-made X-rays. But building there would be very expensive.

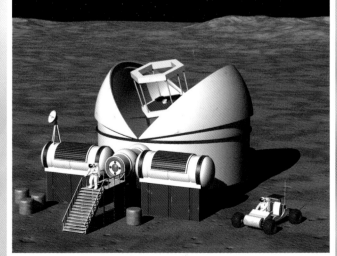

Moon observatory of the future

31

Glossary

Astrology Using patterns in the sky as a guide to daily life.

Astronomy The science of space-watching.

Constellation The pattern that stars seem to make in the sky, from our viewpoint on Earth.

Eclipse When light from the Sun or Moon is blocked out.

Gravity The force of attraction between two objects.

Lens A curved piece of glass.

Observatory A place that houses telescopes and other instruments for viewing the sky.

Orbit The path around a planet or star.

Planet A large body of gas or rock orbiting a star.

Quasar A region of space giving off more energy than almost any other.

Seasons Different times of the year, when Earth's weather and life change according to the position of the Sun in the sky.

Solar panels Mirrors that capture energy from the Sun and turn it into electricity.

Solar System Our Sun and everything that travels around it.

Star A huge ball of super-hot gas.

Telescope An instrument that makes distant objects seem bigger and nearer. They collect light, radio waves, X-rays or other waves.

32

Index

Aristotle 11
astrolabes 14, 15
astrologers 13
astronomers 4–5, 9, 11, 13, 14, 18, 19, 20, 23, 25, 26, 29

Babylonians 8–9, 21
binoculars 5
black holes 26

Chandra X-ray Observatory 28, 29, 30
constellations 8, 11, 12–13
Copernicus, Nicolaus 18, 19

eclipses 6, 8, 10, 11
Egyptians 6, 7
Europa 31

galaxies 22, 25
Galileo 18, 19
gravity 26
Greeks 10–11

Hubble Space Telescope 29

Jupiter 5, 19, 31

Kitt Peak Observatory 21

lenses 16, 17
light years 23
Lippershey, Hans 16, 19

meteors 5
Milky Way 7, 25
Moon, the 5, 9, 10, 11, 31

Newton, Isaac 16, 17
neutrinos 27

observatories 20–21, 28, 31
Orion 13

pole stars 15
pyramids 6

quasars 29

radio telescopes 24–25

sailors 11, 14, 15
satellites 9, 31
seasons 19
Solar System 9, 22, 25
space probes 30, 31
standard candles 22
stars 4, 5, 9, 12, 14, 15, 22–23
Stonehenge 6
Sun 6, 10, 12, 14, 15, 18, 29
Super Kamiokande 27

telescopes 4, 5, 16–17, 19, 20, 21, 23, 24–25, 26–27, 28–29, 30, 31

Very Large Arrays 24, 25, 31

ziggurats 21
zodiac 12, 13